World Safari

L. L. Owens

W9-BRE-458

Contents

Rigby®

A Harcourt Achieve Imprint

www.Rigby.com
1-800-531-5015

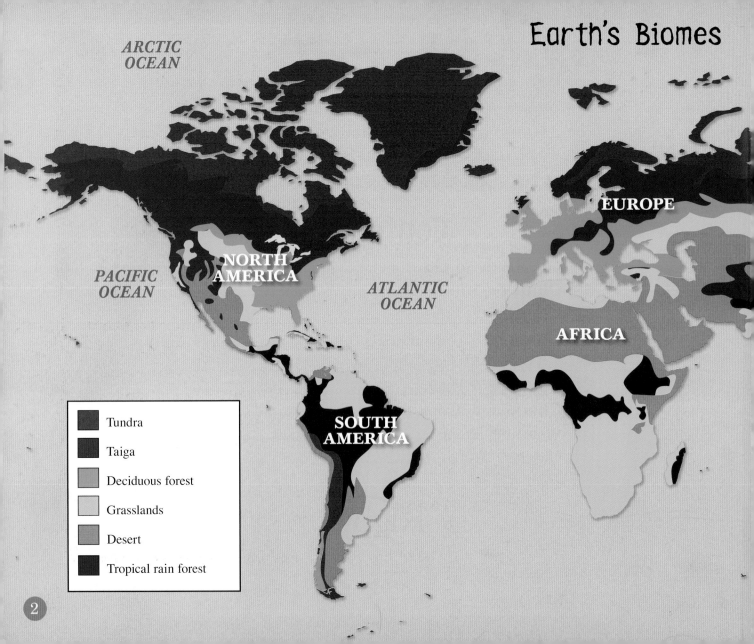

Earth's Biomes

ARCTIC OCEAN

EUROPE

NORTH AMERICA

PACIFIC OCEAN

ATLANTIC OCEAN

AFRICA

SOUTH AMERICA

Tundra

Taiga

Deciduous forest

Grasslands

Desert

Tropical rain forest

ASIA

PACIFIC
OCEAN

INDIAN
OCEAN

AUSTRALIA

Get Ready to Go

Grab your backpack, binoculars, and camera, and get ready to travel deep into the forests, deserts, and grasslands of the world. You are going on a safari through Earth's different **biomes**. Each biome is unique because of its climate and the plants and animals that live there.

Look at the map to see the six major biomes that you'll visit: tundra, taiga, deciduous forest, grasslands, desert, and tropical rain forest. In each biome you'll observe the breathtaking scenery and some of the plants and animals that live there.

Are you ready for your adventure? Great! Let's go!

Chapter 1
Tundra

The first stop on your safari is the tundra. In the northern hemisphere, the tundra covers all of Greenland and the most northern parts of Europe, Asia, and North America.

It's always a good idea to get familiar with a new place, so let's stop and take a look around. What do you notice about the land? You can see that you're in a treeless plain, and the land is almost flat.

Brrrrrrr! It's cold here, so it's good that you packed your warm clothes! If you touch the ground, you'll notice that it feels cold.

The soil just below the surface of the ground is always frozen because of the low temperatures and long winters in the tundra. The wind can be very strong, and in the fall and winter, the sun doesn't rise for several months.

What's the Temperature?

Location	Average Temperature in January	Average Temperature in July
Inuvik, Canada	-21°F	55°F

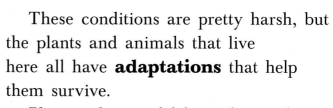

These conditions are pretty harsh, but the plants and animals that live here all have **adaptations** that help them survive.

Plant and animal life in the tundra includes different kinds of mosses and shrubs, as well as animals such as the snowy owl, Arctic fox, and reindeer.

Reindeer have thick fur that gets thinner when the weather is warmer.

What Is an Adaptation?

An adaptation helps a plant or animal survive in its environment. Adaptations can include body parts, such as a reindeer's antlers or a camel's hump. Adaptations also include behavior. For example, bears will mostly sleep through the winter because food is scarce.

What kinds of adaptations do you think would help plants and animals live in the mostly cold and dry tundra?

Take a Closer Look

Have you ever seen reindeer moss? It's very common in the tundra. It's a bushy plant that has many branches, and it can cover large areas of barren land. Reindeer moss doesn't grow very high, and it's not easily damaged by frost, which helps it survive in the tundra. Both animals and humans feed on it, so that makes it especially important.

Look quickly to your left to see the reindeer! The reindeer is a member of the deer family, and in many regions of the world, it's called *caribou*. Notice the reindeer's antlers and large hooves. These help the animal push away the snow to find food hiding underneath.

During the winter, the arctic ground squirrel **hibernates** in its nest deep below the snow. The animal rolls itself into a tight ball, and its body temperature drops to below freezing. There it will stay and sleep for many months. By hibernating underground, the arctic ground squirrel can survive the tundra winters and save up energy for the spring.

Chapter 2
Taiga

Are you ready for a change of scenery? Let's visit the biome called the taiga. The taiga covers a large region south of the tundra in North America, Europe, and Asia.

One of the first things you'll notice is that there are trees as far as you can see! How does it feel to be in the forest? Can you smell the crisp, woody scent of pine needles? Evergreen trees such as pine, spruce, and fir are everywhere since they can survive the taiga's long winters.

Though the winters are long in the taiga, the climate does change throughout the year. In fact, many animals come to the taiga in summer because the weather is warmer, the plants begin growing, and there's plenty to eat.

Some animals, such as bears, live in the taiga year-round, while others, such as certain birds and warm-weather insects, come and go with the seasons.

What's the Temperature?

Location	Average Temperature in January	Average Temperature in July
Fairbanks, Alaska, United States	-6°F	62°F

Take a Closer Look

The most important adaptation for the trees in the taiga is their needles. The Douglas fir has long, thin, waxy needles. The waxy covering helps the needles store water and protects the tree from the cold. And the needles' dark green color helps the tree absorb heat from the sun.

Look down at the ground, and you will see a carpet of pine needles. Unlike trees that lose their leaves in winter, evergreens don't lose all their needles at once. They slowly drop and regrow their needles throughout the year, and some needles may stay on a tree for two years or longer! By keeping their needles, evergreens don't have to use up energy to regrow them in the spring.

Douglas firs can grow up to 60 feet tall and 25 feet wide.

The black bear uses its sharp claws to scrape the bark of the Douglas fir so that it can eat the sap underneath. In the summer, black bears eat a lot and store up fat in their bodies. When winter comes, and food is scarce, the black bear sleeps most of the time in a den, which protects it from the cold.

If you look a little to your right, you'll see a snowshoe hare. It looks brown now, but in the winter the hare's fur turns white. Predators, which are animals that hunt other animals for food, cannot see the hare when it's white because it's the same color as the snow. This type of adaptation is called **camouflage**.

Camouflage is an animal's color or pattern that helps it blend in with its environment. Can you think of any other animals that use camouflage to survive?

Chapter 3
Deciduous Forest

Crunch, crunch, crunch, crunch. . . . That's the sound you hear as you walk through piles of fallen leaves. Now you are in the deciduous forest. You're in eastern Asia, western or central Europe, or eastern North America. And it must be fall because that's when the air turns brisk and broad-leaved deciduous trees, such as the maple and oak, prepare for winter by shedding their leaves. *Deciduous* means "to fall off, or shed, with the seasons," and all deciduous trees lose their leaves each year.

So why *do* deciduous trees lose their leaves? The trees in a deciduous forest change with each season. Winter is very dry, and there's not enough water to support the leaves. So the trees shed their leaves and stay inactive until spring and summer, when they begin to grow again. The leaves on deciduous trees are lightweight and broad, which helps them easily absorb sunlight.

What's the Temperature?

Location	Average Temperature in January	Average Temperature in July
Staunton, Virginia, United States	30°F	72°F

Take a Closer Look

Look closely, and you'll notice three layers of plant life in the deciduous forest, with tall trees forming the top layer. The second layer is made up of shrubs and shorter trees, and a layer of ferns and mosses grows close to the ground. These layers create the ideal environment for many animals. The trees are far enough apart so that sunlight can get through the top layer. That means that the other two layers of trees and plants get the sun that they need to grow.

Can you see those deer eating grass over there? You could have easily missed them since their fur blends in so well with the brush. We don't want to startle them, so try not to make any sudden movements or loud noises.

One of the deer's behavioral adaptations is its **instinct** to stand perfectly still when it feels threatened. An instinct is a behavior that an animal is born with. The deer knows that if it stands very still, certain enemies will ignore it and think it's part of the brush.

Look over there to see the eastern chipmunk that's nibbling on something. Eastern chipmunks live in the northeastern United States and southeastern Canada.

They carry nuts and seeds in their cheeks, which are like pouches. The chipmunk has adapted to the cold winter by storing food. In the fall, when there are many nuts and seeds on the ground, the chipmunk collects food and buries it underground in a nest. When winter comes, the chipmunk then stays underground and eats the food that it has buried.

Look at that walking stick on a twig over there! It's hard to see because it looks just like the twig. Walking sticks are insects that have an adaptation called **mimicry**.

Mimicry is an adaptation in which an animal looks just like another animal or an object. Walking sticks look just like twigs and branches, so it is difficult for predators to see them.

Chapter 4
Grasslands

Now you are entering the grasslands. You can guess where this biome got its name, can't you? Almost all the plants you see here are grasses. You might be in the prairies of North America.

If you grab your binoculars, you can probably survey the land and spot some of the animals living here, such as rats, snakes, prairie dogs, and bison.

Grasslands are dry and have hot summers, cold winters, and short growing seasons. Grasslands are very important for people, too. All over the world they are used for growing crops, such as corn and wheat, and as grazing fields for cattle and sheep.

What's the Temperature?

Location	Average Temperature in January	Average Temperature in July
Wichita, Kansas, United States	30°F	81°F

Grasses are strong plants, and they spread quickly because their seeds are easily carried by the wind or by animals. They have roots that spread out just below the surface of the soil. The roots can find water even during a drought, when there hasn't been any rain for a long time. The grasses' long, narrow leaves also help prevent water loss.

Of course you won't be surprised to see a grasshopper living in the grasslands. Its color helps it blend in as it eats the grass and lays its eggs on the ground.

The wild turkey can run fast, and it has fantastic eyesight, so catching grasshoppers and finding the clover that it likes to eat is easy. Because there are so few trees, this bird seeks shelter in the tall grasses. It has to watch out for predators such as the coyote.

Another animal that the coyote preys on is the bison. Millions of bison used to roam parts of Canada and the United States. But because so many bison were hunted and killed, there are only 50,000 remaining in the United States today. These bison now live in parks and game reserves.

Bison eat grass, and they grow thick, heavy fur that keeps them warm in the winter. When the weather gets warmer, bison shed their fur to stay cool.

Chapter 5

Desert

Can you feel the air getting drier and drier? Now you're stepping into the desert biome. Go ahead and have a drink of water—you're going to need it!

You can find deserts on every continent in the world. All deserts are dry and most get less than 10 inches of rainfall per year. Though many deserts are hot, you might be surprised to learn that there are cold deserts, too.

Comparing Deserts

	Hot and Dry Desert	Cold Desert
Locations	• Australia, North America, Africa, southern Asia, and South and Central America	• Greenland, Antarctica, northwest China, Mongolia, and Chile
Climate	• Warm all year • Hot summers • Less than 10 inches of rain each year	• Cold winters with snow • 6-11 inches of rain each year
Plants	• Small shrubs and cacti	• Tall shrubs and some trees
Kinds of Animals	• Reptiles, coyotes, foxes, owls, and hawks	• Jackrabbits, kangaroo rats, lizards, and coyotes

Take a Closer Look

What's one of the first things you look for when you're out in the hot sun and you want to cool off? You look for some shade, of course! During the day, the sun is intense, and shade can be hard to find in the desert. The ant, like other insects in the desert, will spend the day avoiding the heat by simply changing positions on a twig. When the sun hits its back, the ant will move.

The snakes and lizards that inhabit the desert all have tough, scaly skin that prevents them from losing water. And many other desert animals simply hide during the day and only come out at night, when it is cooler.

Water is very scarce in the desert, so desert plants and animals have adaptations that help them survive without much water. The cactus plant stores water in its stem, so it can survive long periods without rain. Also its roots stay close to the soil's surface so they can quickly absorb any rain that might fall.

What's the Temperature?

Location	Average Temperature in January	Average Temperature in July
Chihuahua, Mexico	54°F	78°F

The dromedary camel lives in the deserts of North Africa, and it actually stores water in its body. When a camel has not had water for a long time, its body uses the fat in its hump for water. A camel can survive for months without water, but when it finally refreshes itself with a drink, it can drink up to 50 gallons!

A camel's long, thick eyelashes are another adaptation to living in the desert. Its eyelashes protect its eyes from the blowing sand and the sun's glare.

Dromedary camels also have thick pads on their knees that are useful when kneeling. People can load packs or climb onto a camel's back when it is kneeling.

Chapter 6
Tropical Rain Forest

Can you feel it getting humid? It feels like it's going to rain. You might have already guessed that we're heading into the wet, lush, green biome called the tropical rain forest. Before we go any farther, grab your hat and put on your sunglasses. You can be sure that you'll get wet, and the rain combined with periods of strong sunshine can sometimes make it hard to see in the rain forest.

The tropical rain forest is the wettest of all the biomes. Some rain forests get more than 100 inches of rain each year. The heavy rainfall and sunshine support an incredible variety of plant and animal life. In fact, more than half of the world's plant and animal species can be found in the tropical rain forest.

The tropical rain forest is found in much of Africa and in parts of Central and South America. It's also found in Southeast Asia, northeast Australia, and the East Indies. All of these warm, wet regions are located near the equator.

Take a Closer Look

Like the deciduous forest, the tropical rain forest is also made up of many trees. One difference is that the trees in the rain forest have longer, straighter trunks and no branches until a height of about 100 feet. And unlike deciduous trees, which have thick bark that helps retain water and protects them from the cold, trees in the tropical rain forest have smooth, thin bark. There is no need for protection against cold temperatures in the tropical rain forest.

What's the Temperature?		
Location	Average Temperature in January	Average Temperature in July
Manaus, Brazil	80°F	80°F

You'll notice that there are four layers in the rain forest. In the top layer, or the canopy, are the tops of giant trees that reach more than 150 feet high.

Below this layer is the sub-canopy. Most of the rain forest's animals live here. In fact, some animals spend their whole lives in the sub-canopy.

The next layer down is the understory, which is a shady, lower area that is made up of shrubs and small trees. Less than 1% of the sunlight in the rain forest reaches the understory.

Finally you reach the forest floor, which is bare except for some dead leaves and plants. Very few plants can grow on the forest floor because there is so little light, and the layer of soil is very thin.

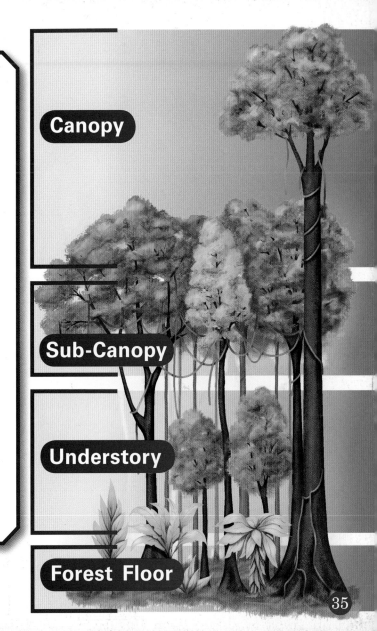

Canopy

Sub-Canopy

Understory

Forest Floor

Now look way up in the treetops, and you'll see the striking, brightly colored scarlet macaw. The bird's sharp, hooked beak helps it crack open nuts, defend itself against other animals, and climb trees. (The macaw uses its beak as a third foot.)

Can you see the spider monkey that is hanging from a branch by its tail? Since the spider monkey spends its entire life in the sub-canopy of the rain forest, it uses its long tail as another arm to swing from tree to tree.

You'll also see that there are lots of vines climbing the trees. Vines have adapted to living in the rain forest by using other plants and trees for support and climbing toward the sunlight.

Welcome Home

You've done it! You've completed your safari through the six major biomes on Earth. Along the way you saw some incredible places and the plants and animals that live in each biome. It's time to unpack your binoculars and camera. Soon you'll be able to look at your photographs and remember all the wonderful things you saw. It has been a real adventure!

Glossary

adaptation body parts, plant parts, or animal behavior that help a plant or animal survive in its environment

biome a large area on Earth with a specific climate and plants and animals

camouflage an animal's color or pattern that helps it blend in with its environment

hibernate to go into a long, deep sleep during winter

instinct a behavior that an animal is born with

mimicry an adaptation in which an animal looks like another animal or an object

Index